George Washington Carver
A Photo Biography

by John Riley, M.Ed.

First Biographies
an Imprint of Morgan Reynolds, Inc.

Greensboro

George Washington Carver: A Photo Biography

Copyright © 2000 by John Riley

Photo credits: Tuskegee University Archives

Library of Congress Cataloging-in-Publication Data

Riley, John, 1955-
   George Washington Carver : a photo-biography / by John Riley.-- 1st ed.
      p. cm.
   Includes bibliographical references (p.) and index.
   Summary: A simple biography of George Washington Carver, the founder of the
Tuskegee Institue.
   ISBN 1-883846-62-5
   1. Carver, George Washington, 1864?-1943--Juvenile literature. 2. Afro-American
agriculturists--Biography--Juvenile literature. 3. Agriculturists--United
States--Biography--Juvenile literature. [1. Carver, George Washington, 1864?-1943. 2.
Agriculturists. 3. Afro-Americans--Biography.] I. Title.

S417.C3 R46 2000
630'.92--dc21
[B]
                                                              99-089220

Printed in the United States of America

First Edition

Table of Contents

Boldface words are defined in **Words to Know**.

A Better World

George Washington Carver learned all he could about plants. He became a teacher. He helped farmers grow more food.

George thought all people should be treated equally.

Many thought George was the greatest scientist in the world. He became famous. George said he was only trying to make people's lives better.

Many people thought George was the world's greatest scientist.

Childhood

George Washington Carver was born in 1865. His parents died when he was a child.

George lived on a farm. He liked to spend time in the woods. He collected frogs and different types of plants.

George liked to read and learn. But he had a problem. Few schools would teach African-American children.

George left home to find a school. He was 12 years old.

George was a talented boy.

Traveling Man

George traveled for twelve years. He attended several schools. Science and art were his favorite subjects.

Then George became a **homesteader**. He built a house. He planted corn and other vegetables.

Life as a homesteader was hard. There was snow in the winter. There was not enough rain in the summer.

George left his farm in 1889. He moved to Iowa.

George worked as a farmer. Then he went back to school.

Life in College

George went to college. He studied **agriculture**.

George liked to make new plants. One way to do this was by joining two plants together. The new plant was called a **hybrid**.

In 1896 George moved to Alabama. He became a teacher at a school for African Americans. It was called the Tuskegee Institute.

George liked to paint flowers.

Teacher at Tuskegee

Booker T. Washington was the president of Tuskegee Institute. He wanted to help African-American students get better jobs.

George taught agriculture. He took students on field trips to look at plants up close. He said this was the best way to learn new things.

George did **experiments** on **crops**. He wrote down what he learned into books. The books helped farmers grow better crops.

Booker T. Washington wanted to help African Americans learn new skills.

Helping Farmers

George wanted to help farmers. He spoke at meetings and talked to farmers in their fields. The farmers used his advice to raise more food.

George met the inventor Thomas A. Edison. Edison wanted George to work with him. He offered to pay George lots of money. George said no. He wanted to stay at Tuskegee.

Students and farmers liked to listen to George's lectures.

Working for Peanuts

George made dozens of new products from peanuts. He said the peanut was a wonderful plant.

George spoke to the leaders of the United States. They asked him about his work with the peanut.

Newspapers wrote stories about the peanut scientist. More people asked him to give speeches.

George found new ways to use the peanut.

Famous Scientist

George wanted all people to live together peacefully. He asked young people to always be kind to others.

Henry Ford was a very wealthy man. He said that George was "the world's greatest living scientist."

George made new products. He made medicines to fight diseases. He started a company to sell his products.

George's life was made into a movie. He played himself as an old man.

Henry Ford believed George was a great scientist.

Honors for a Life's Work

George spoke at many colleges. But he liked working in his **laboratory** best.

Tuskegee opened the George Washington Carver Museum. His equipment is inside the **museum**.

George died on January 5, 1943. He was 77 years old. He is buried at the Tuskegee Institute.

George's birthplace is a national **monument**. You can visit it today.

The George Washington Carver Museum is located in Tuskegee, Alabama.

Timeline

1865—George Washington Carver is born.

1877—Leaves home.

1890—Accepted to Iowa State College.

1896—Begins working at Tuskegee Institute.

1921—Talks to Congress about the peanut.

1941—George Washington Carver Museum opens.

1943—George dies.

Words to Know

agriculture: [AG-ruh-kull-chur] raising plants and farm animals for food.

crops: [KROPS] plants grown for food.

experiments: [ex-PEER-uh-ments] tests used for making discoveries.

homesteader: [HOME-sted-ur] a person who claims a piece of land to live and farm on.

hybrid: [HI-brid] a plant made from two other plants.

laboratory: [LAB-ruh-tour-ee] a room used for practicing science.

museum: [mew-ZEE-um] a building where important old objects are kept.

monument: [MON-u-ment] a special building or statue that stands for a person or event.

Further Reading

Adair, Gene. *George Washington Carver*. Chelsea House Publishers. New York, 1989.

Eliot, Lawrence. *George Washington Carver: The Man Who Overcame*. Prentice-Hall. Englewood Cliffs, NJ, 1966.

Kremer, Gary R. *George Washington Carver: In His Own Words*. University of Missouri Press. Columbia, 1986.

Websites

George Washington Carver National Monument in Diamond, Missouri:
http://www.nps.gov/gwca/index.htm/

Louisiana State University Library:
http://www.lib.lsu.edu/lib/chem/display/carver.html

Tuskegee Institute:
http://www.nps.gov/bowa/tuskin.html

Places to Write

Tuskegee University Archives
Hollis Burke Frissell Library
Tuskegee, Alabama 36088

Tuskegee Institute National Historic Site
The George Washington Carver Museum
P. O. Drawer 10
Tuskegee Institute, Alabama 36087
(334) 727-6390

Index